Booker T. Washington

Booker T. Washington

by Thomas Amper
illustrations by Jeni Reeves

Carolrhoda Books, Inc./Minneapolis

Thanks to the Hampton University Archives for making the portrait of Booker T. Washington on page 2 possible with the use of their photograph. Special thanks to Noreen Black and Pamela Nosek. Thanks also to the Grafft and Sturges Families and Susan Kuecher. Thanks to these people and organizations: Booker T. Washington National Monument and Rangers Haynes, Colbert, and Sims; Ms. Maupin at Hampton University Archives; Ferrum College; Valentine Museum at Richmond; Library of Virginia; Kanawha County Library, West Virginia; National Coal Museum; The History Center, Masonic Library, and Seminole Valley Farm in Cedar Rapids; and Living History Farms, Des Moines, Iowa.   —J.R.

The photograph on page 47 appears courtesy of the Library of Congress.

This book is available in two editions:
Library binding by Carolrhoda Books, Inc., a division of Lerner Publishing Group
Soft cover by First Avenue Editions, an imprint of Lerner Publishing Group
241 First Avenue North
Minneapolis, MN 55401 U.S.A.

Website address: www.lernerbooks.com

Library of Congress Cataloging-in-Publication Data

Amper, Thomas.
   Booker T. Washington / by Thomas Amper ; illustrations by Jeni Reeves.
      p. cm. — (Carolrhoda on my own books)
   Summary: Tells the story of Booker T. Washington's childhood following the end of slavery, his struggle to get an education, and his journey at age sixteen to the Hampton Institute.
   ISBN-13: 978-1-57505-094-2 (lib. bdg. : alk. paper)
   ISBN-10: 1-57505-094-3 (lib. bdg. : alk. paper)
   ISBN-13: 978-0-87614-534-0 (pbk. : alk. paper)
   ISBN-10: 0-87614-534-9 (pbk. : alk. paper)
   1. Washington, Booker T., 1856–1915—Childhood and youth—Juvenile literature. 2. Afro-Americans—Biography—Juvenile literature. 3. Educators—United States—Biography—Juvenile literature. [1. Washington, Booker T., 1856–1915—Childhood and youth. 2. Educators. 3. Afro-Americans—Biography.] I. Reeves, Jeni, ill. II. Title. III. Series.
E185.97.W4A55 1998
370'.92—dc21   97-27454

Manufactured in the United States of America
5 6 7 8 9 10 – JR – 10 09 08 07 06 05

*In memory of Aunt Sally, who taught
me to believe in magic.*

—*T. A.*

*To my parents, who first sparked
my imagination.*

—*J. R.*

Hale's Ford, Virginia
1863

It was early in the morning.

The road through the woods was dark.

Seven-year-old Booker walked

with Miss Ellen to school.

He carried her books.

When they got to the school,

Miss Ellen went in.

Booker went home.

He was a slave.

It was against the law

for slaves to go to school.

Booker lived on a farm in Virginia.
As a slave, he had to do
what his master wanted.
Miss Ellen was the master's daughter.
Sometimes Booker carried her books.
More often, he carried water to the men
working in the fields.

Booker wished he could go to school.

He had watched

the white boys and girls in school.

He wanted to sit at a desk

and bend over a book.

He wanted to find the answer to a question

and tell the whole class.

He wanted to look at a sign or a newspaper

and tell people what the black letters said.

When Booker was nine years old,

a man came to the farm.

The slaves were called to listen to him.

Booker stood with his mother,

his brother, and his sister.

The man said that the Civil War was over.

The slaves were now free.

People began shouting with excitement.

Booker's mother leaned down

and kissed her children.

She had prayed for this day, she said.

Booker's family soon left the farm

and moved to West Virginia.

They were ready to start

a new life of freedom.

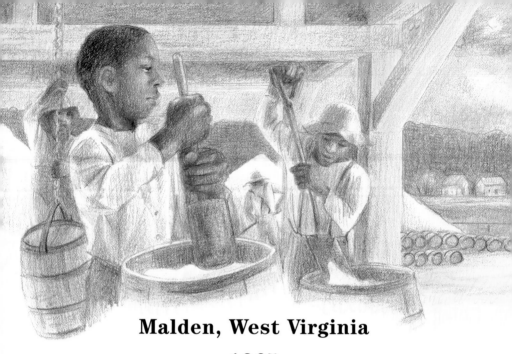

Malden, West Virginia
1865

For Booker, freedom meant one thing.

Now he could go to school.

His stepfather had a different idea.

The family was poor,

and they needed money.

Booker's stepfather took Booker

and his brother to work at a salt mine.

They shoveled salt into barrels.

Then they pounded it down.

The work was hard and heavy.

They started at four o'clock in the morning,

and they worked until after dark.

The worst part was what Booker could see.

From where he worked,

he saw boys and girls walking to school.

Booker wished he were with them.

Booker decided to teach himself.

He learned the alphabet from a book.

Soon his mother spoke to the teacher
at the school.

The teacher agreed to help Booker
at night, after work.

Booker studied hard and learned fast.

But he still wanted to go to a real school
with other children.

When Booker was about twelve,
he went to work in a coal mine.
He dug coal in underground tunnels.
The mine was dark and terrifying.
At any moment, it could cave in
or even explode.
Booker often brought a book into the mine.
Whenever he found a chance,
he studied the book.

One day in the dark mine,
Booker heard two men talking.
They spoke about a new school
for African Americans.
It was called the Hampton Institute.
Boys could go there
even if they did not have money.
They could work at the school
to pay their way.

The men spoke softly,
but their words rang in Booker's heart.
He didn't know where Hampton was,
or how to get there.
He only knew that somehow
he would go to this school.

Booker asked his parents if he could go
to Hampton, but they said no.
They still needed the money he earned.
So Booker kept working in the mine
and studying at night.
A few months later,
Booker heard about a job.
Mrs. Viola Ruffner needed a servant.
Booker had heard that she was very strict,
but he wanted to get out of the mine.
So he took the job.

Mrs. Ruffner turned out to be
as strict as people said.
When Booker swept the floor,
she said it was not good enough.
He had missed some dirt in the corners.
When Booker raked the lawn,
she said it was not good enough.
She showed him where he had left
narrow strips of leaves.

One day Mrs. Ruffner told Booker
to weed the garden.
At first, he worked quickly.
He pulled up a dandelion here
and some grass there.
When he was done, he paused.

Booker did not want to go to Mrs. Ruffner.

He knew what she would say.

So he pretended he was Mrs. Ruffner.

He pointed out everything that was wrong.

He saw some grass and weeds
he had missed.

He pulled them up.

He also saw some papers and twigs
on the ground.
Mrs. Ruffner had not said
anything about papers and twigs.
But Booker picked them up, too.

Booker could hardly wait
to show Mrs. Ruffner.
But first, he carefully went over
the garden one more time.
It looked perfect.
When Mrs. Ruffner saw the garden,
a strange thing happened.
The mean Mrs. Ruffner was gone.
From then on, she was friendly and kind.
She praised Booker's work.
Sometimes she even let him
go to school in the afternoon,
if he got his work done in the morning.

Booker was different now, too.
He worked a little harder
at everything he did.
In fact, he even liked to work.
Mrs. Ruffner had taught Booker
the most important lesson of his life.

Booker now liked his job,
but he still kept dreaming
of the school in Hampton.
Finally, when he was 16,
his mother said he could go.

But getting to Hampton would not be easy.
First, Booker needed money
for clothes and travel.
He had saved a little.
His brother gave him a little bit more.
Then people all over town started
giving him money.

They all wanted to help him,
even though they were poor, too.
Most of them had been slaves.
They had never had an education.
They were proud that
one of their own people
was going away to school.

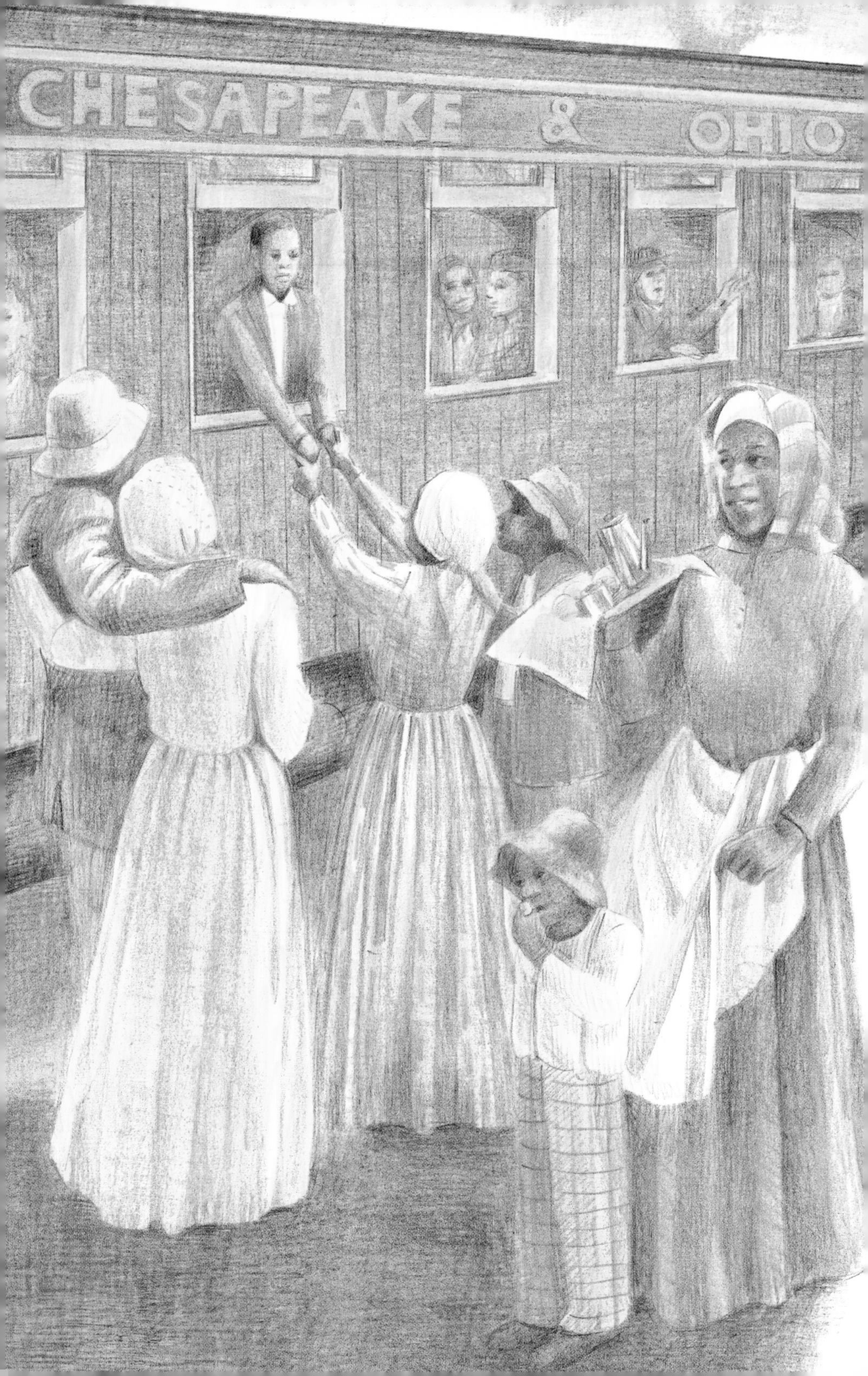
CHESAPEAKE & OHIO

Fall 1872

When the day came for Booker to leave,
he felt excited and proud.
He was not going to school alone.
He was taking the hopes
of his people with him.
Booker also felt sad.
His mother was sick,
and he was afraid he would never
see her again.

Hampton was 500 miles away in Virginia.

At first, Booker took a train.

Then he rode in a stagecoach.

But he didn't have much money.

So he began to walk.

Day after day he traveled.

Sometimes he got rides in passing wagons.

At night, he slept in fields along the road.

He got tired and hungry,

but he kept on going.

Booker traveled for more than two weeks.

Late one night,

he reached the city of Richmond.

He was just 80 miles from Hampton.

He needed a place to stay,

but all his money was gone.

He offered to work to pay for a room.

Everyone turned him away.

Booker walked the streets.

He had never seen a city before.

Everything seemed strange.

The people looked and sounded
different from the people back home.

He thought about the friends who had placed
their hopes in him.

He did not feel proud now.

He felt scared and alone.

Booker kept walking.
He grew so tired that he could
barely take another step.
Then, just ahead, he saw a space
under the boards of the sidewalk.
When no one was looking,
he scooted underneath.
He curled up like a caterpillar
and tried to sleep.

The sounds of footsteps boomed
down on him all through the night.
Booker wondered who had made
the night so long.
At last the black sky began to brighten.
Booker arose.

Booker needed money for food
and for the rest of his trip to Hampton.
He walked down to the river.
There he found a job helping unload a ship.
The work was hard, but Booker felt strong.
Soon I'll be at Hampton, he told himself.

He worked on the ship for several days.
Each night, he slept under the sidewalk
to save money.
Finally, he had enough.
Booker took a stagecoach
the rest of the way to Hampton.

When he got to Hampton,
Booker quickly found the school.
He looked up at the red brick building.
It seemed like the most beautiful
building in the world.

But Booker's problems were not over yet.
He had to ask the head teacher
to accept him into the school.
Booker knew how messy he looked.
He had traveled 500 miles.
He had not taken a bath
or changed his clothes for weeks.

Booker found the head teacher.

Her name was Miss Mackie.

She looked him over and frowned.

She told him to wait.

Hours went by.

Other boys came and were accepted.

Booker kept waiting.

His heart began to sink.

Finally, Miss Mackie handed him a broom.
She told him to sweep
the classroom next door.
Booker jumped to his feet,
took the broom, and hurried away.
He knew he was good at sweeping.
After working for Mrs. Ruffner,
he was an expert.

Booker swept the floor three times.

He wiped it with a dust rag.

Then he carefully dusted all the desks,

all the woodwork,

and every corner of the room.

He found Miss Mackie

and told her he was done.

Away she marched to the classroom,
with Booker right behind.
Miss Mackie walked around the room.
In the afternoon sun,
the woodwork gleamed.
The desks glowed.
Miss Mackie stopped at the door.
She took out a handkerchief.
Then she ran it along the top
of the doorframe.

She looked at the handkerchief.

There was not a speck of dust on it.

A tiny smile crossed her face.

"I guess you will do

to enter this institution," she said.

Booker's face lit up

with happiness and pride.

His dream had finally come true.

Tomorrow morning, he was going to school.

Afterword

Booker T. Washington went to Hampton for three years. He then became a teacher of other African-American students. He taught in his hometown for two years and then at the Hampton Institute.

In 1881, Booker was chosen to be the principal of a new school for African Americans in Alabama. Under Booker's leadership, the Tuskegee Institute grew into one of the most famous schools in America.

With the success of Tuskegee, Booker became a famous leader of African Americans. He was a great public speaker, and he traveled all over America. He spoke about education and about how African Americans and white Americans could get along. Booker T. Washington will always be remembered as a great American teacher and leader.

Important Dates

1856—Booker T. Washington is born in Hale's Ford, Virginia. (His exact date of birth is unknown.)

1865—Moves with his family to Malden, West Virginia

1872–1875—Attends school at the Hampton Institute

1875—Graduates from Hampton and returns to Malden to teach school

1879—Begins teaching at Hampton

1881—Opens the Tuskegee Institute in Tuskegee, Alabama

1882—Marries Fannie Smith

1883—Daughter Portia is born

1884—Fannie Washington dies

1885—Marries second wife, Olivia Davidson; son Booker T. Jr. is born

1889—Son Ernest Davidson is born; Olivia Washington dies

1892—Marries third wife, Margaret Murray

1895—Delivers his famous Atlanta Compromise speech in Atlanta, Georgia

1900—Founds National Negro Business League

1901—Publishes his autobiography, *Up from Slavery*

1915—Died on November 13 in Tuskegee, Alabama